The Beginning of the Renaissance

History Book for Kids 9-12

Children's Renaissance Books

Speedy Publishing LLC

40 E. Main St. #1156

Newark, DE 19711

www.speedypublishing.com

Copyright 2017

In this book, we're going to talk about the beginning of the Renaissance. So, let's get right to it!

The Renaissance period of European history was from 1300 AD to 1700 AD and began in Italy. At the beginning of this period, the country of Italy was divided into regions of land called city-states. The reason they were called this is because a large city was the powerful center of each region.

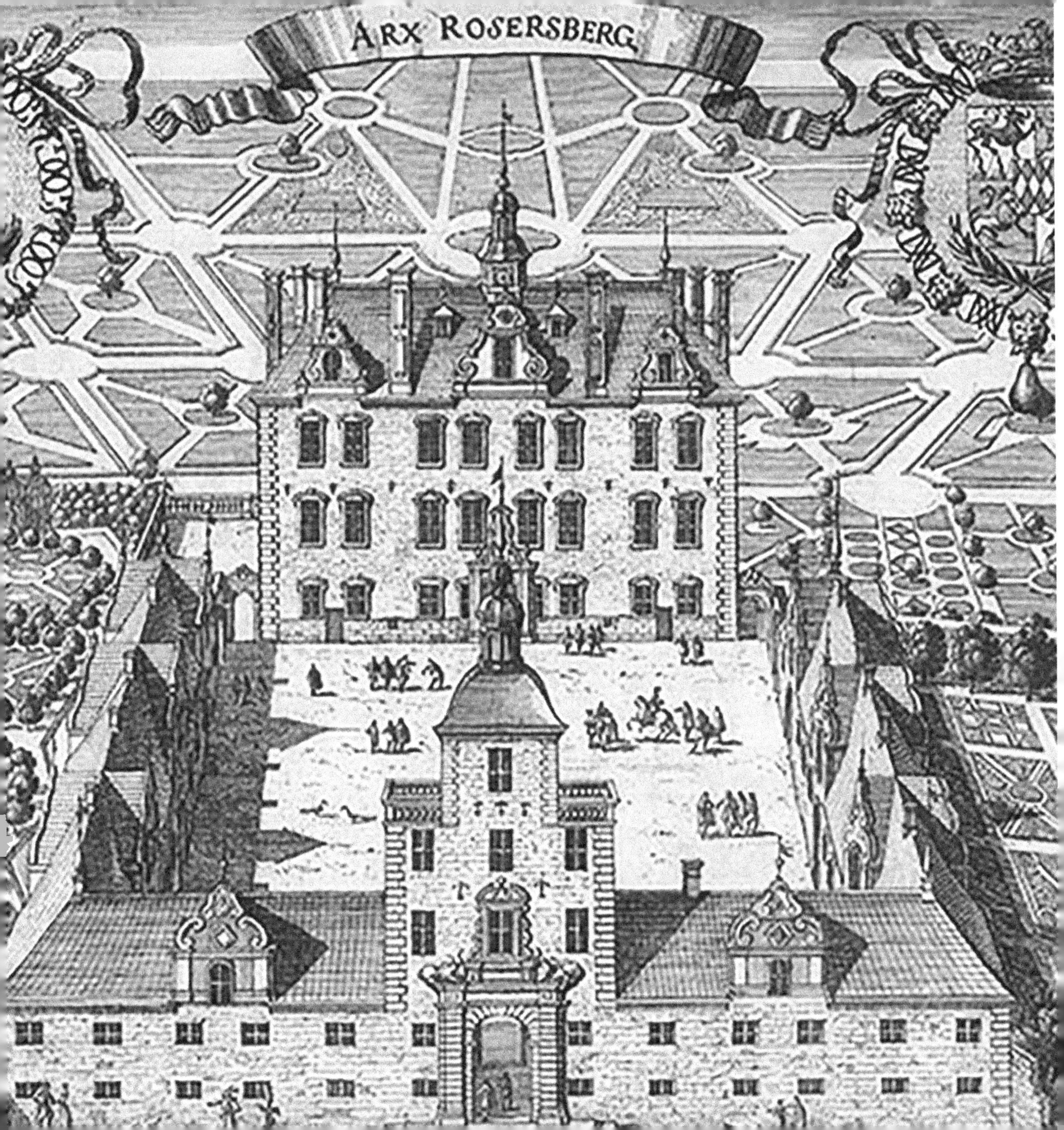

ARX ROSERSBERG

FLORENCE

Instead of being ruled by one central government, each city-state had its own government. One of these important city-states was the region of Florence. The government there was set up as a republic and operated much like the government of Ancient Rome had operated. The citizens chose their own rulers.

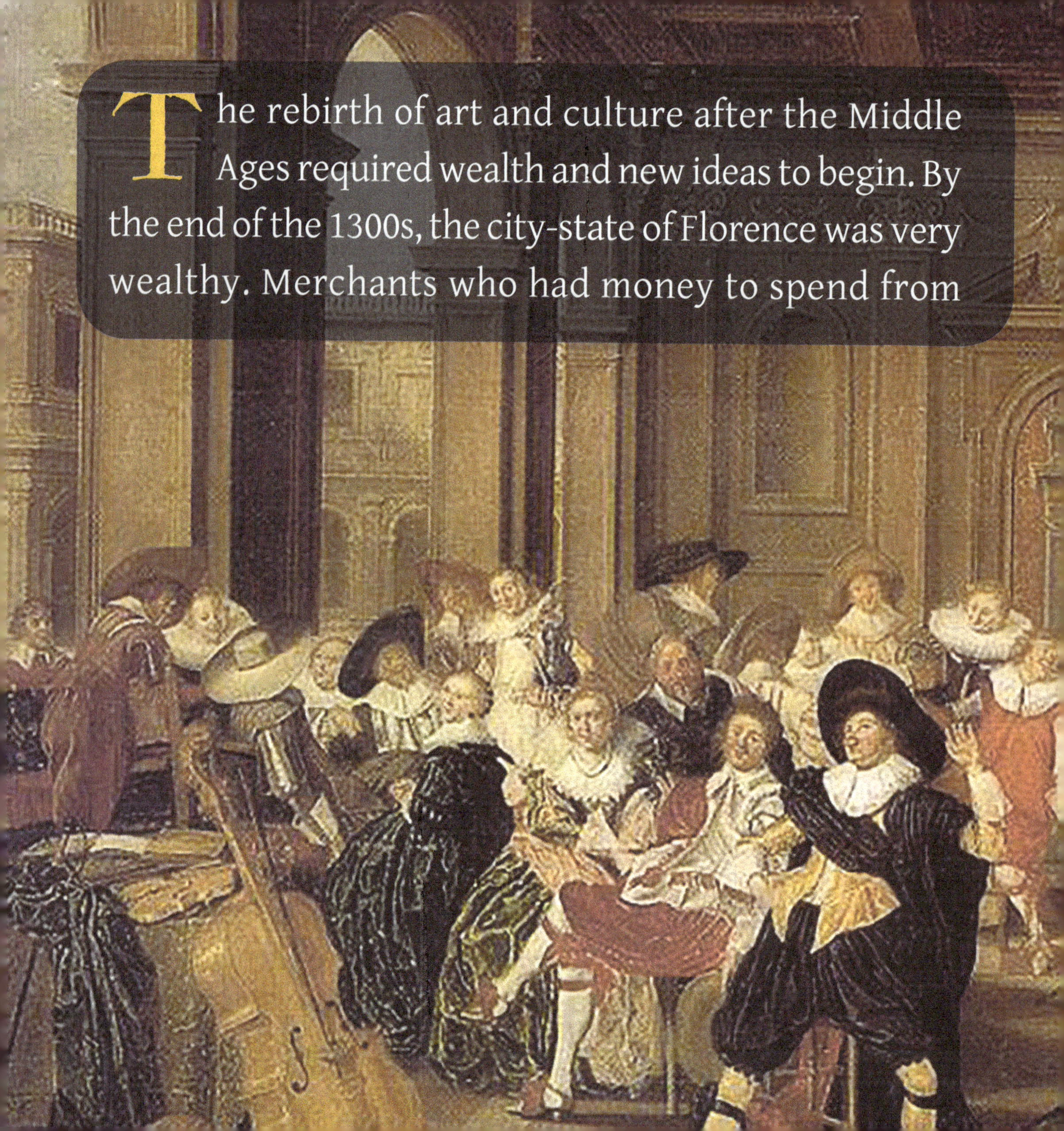

The rebirth of art and culture after the Middle Ages required wealth and new ideas to begin. By the end of the 1300s, the city-state of Florence was very wealthy. Merchants who had money to spend from

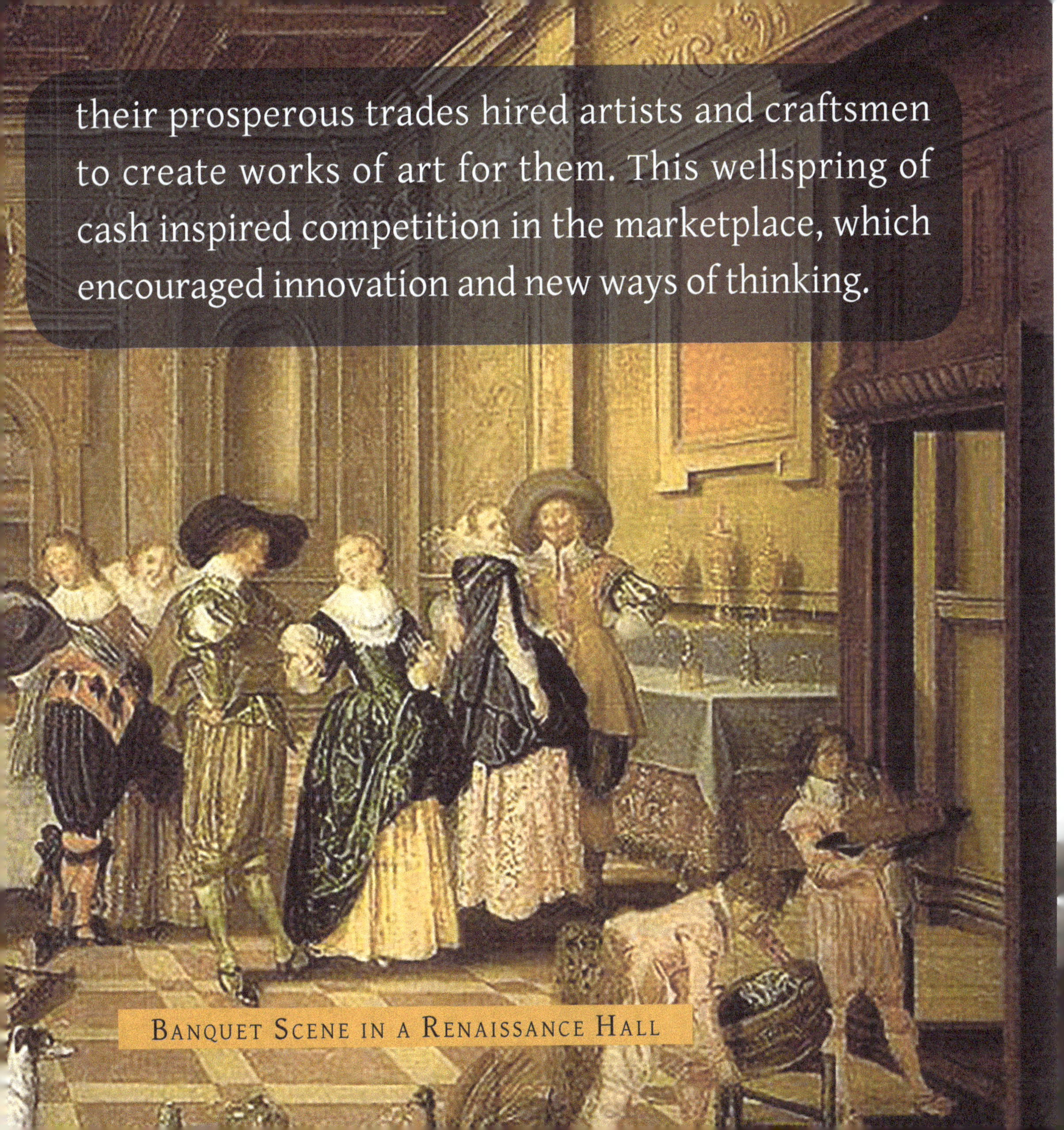

their prosperous trades hired artists and craftsmen to create works of art for them. This wellspring of cash inspired competition in the marketplace, which encouraged innovation and new ways of thinking.

THE HUMANIST MOVEMENT

The Humanist movement was a cultural change that occurred at the beginning of the Renaissance. Prior to the Renaissance, during the time of the Middle Ages from 476 AD to 1400 AD, life in Europe had been filled with suffering, war, and disease.

MIDDLE AGES

BLACK DEATH

In the years between 1347 AD and 1352 AD over 25 million people, about one-third of Europe's population died of the Black Death. Because of these experiences, people who lived in the Middle Ages thought that everyday life was destined to be filled with hardship.

As the city-state of Florence became more prosperous in the late 1300s and 1400s, the population there began to think differently about daily life. They realized through their studies that life didn't have to be this way. They studied the ancient civilizations of the Greeks and Romans and realized that the life style had been better during those earlier periods of history.

Florence

They began to turn away from the medieval scholasticism, which concentrated on the dogma and tradition of the Catholic Church. They wanted to revive the comforts and culture of their earlier ancient ancestors.

The principles of Humanism gave people the freedom to think that life could be filled with pleasure. People should be surrounded by comforts. They should enjoy quality education and their lives

should be filled with the richness of beautiful art, harmonic music, and innovative science. This type of life was so different than what had been experienced by most people during the Middle Ages.

THE CAMPIDOGLIO - RENAISSANCE ARCHITECTURE

TIMELINE OF THE RENAISSANCE

There was about a century of overlap between the time when most of Europe was still experiencing the Middle Ages and the Renaissance was beginning. Today we call this period of time between 1300 AD and 1400 AD the Proto-Renaissance, which simply means the beginning of the Renaissance.

This time period was followed by the Early Renaissance from 1400 AD to 1500 AD, and the High Renaissance from 1495 AD to 1527 AD. Once again, there is an overlap as transitions were made from one period to another.

Renaissance Interior with Banqueters

FRANCESCO PETRARCA

FRANCESCO PETRARCA, THE FATHER OF HUMANISM

Francesco Petrarca was a major influencer during the Proto-Renaissance. He was born in Arezzo, a city in the region of Tuscany in 1304. He was a scholar of the classics and a poet.

A s Petrarca studied more and more about the classical period between the 8th century BC and the 5th century AD, he felt that humanity could once again reach the height of the Greek and Roman culture that had existed then. Petrarca, also called Petrarch, wrote sonnets and histories. He was admired during his lifetime and his ideas as well as his writing provided inspiration for thousands of writers throughout Europe. He was given the honor of becoming Rome's official poet, called the poet laureate, in 1341.

Francesco Petrarca

VIRGIL READING THE AENEID

Because he was one of the first scholars of the classics, Petrarch discovered knowledge that had been hidden for centuries. He studied the classical poets such as Virgil and Cicero. His writings helped spark the focus on Humanism during the Early Renaissance.

A long with Dante Alighieri, the famous writer of The Divine Comedy, his writings provided the foundation for the modern-day language of Italy. Many of his poems and histories were written in the language of ordinary people instead of the more formal scholarly language that Italian writers had used before.

Dante Alighieri

Divine Comedy

DANTE ALIGHIERI AND THE DIVINE COMEDY

Dante Alighieri was born in June of 1265. Dante wrote The Divine Comedy from the years 1308 to 1321 and completed it right before he died. The Divine Comedy is a story set in the afterlife as Dante travels through Hell, then Purgatory, and finally Heaven. It represents the journey a person's soul takes on its travels to God.

This epic poem is considered the greatest work of Italian literature ever written. Like Petrarca, Dante preferred to write in the ordinary language of Italian people. The country of Italy had many different dialects so their work in unifying the word usage and grammar of the Italian language had a long-lasting impact.

Dante's Inferno

CAPPELLA DEGLI SCROVEGNI

GIOTTO DI BONDONE, THE FIRST RENAISSANCE PAINTER

Giotto di Bondone was the first painter to try creating paintings in a very different style than the style that had been commonplace during the Middle Ages. The style in the Middle Ages was called the Byzantine style and it had a look that was religious, flat-looking, and somewhat abstract.

The figures looked like icons. Giotto completely broke away from this tradition. His paintings had a realism that hadn't been seen before. He painted objects and people as they looked when he observed them.

Scrovegni Chapel

This new style of painting with realistic details was the inspiration for the transformation of painting that became Renaissance art. In 1305 AD, Giotto completed one of his masterpiecess—the frescoes on the walls of the Scrovegni Chapel located in Padua.

The frescoes depict stories from the lives of the Virgin Mary and Christ. One of the famous panels is called The Adoration of the Magi. It shows the star of Bethlehem streaking across the sky like a comet as the three wise men come to worship the baby Jesus.

FLIGHT INTO EGYPT

One of the features that sets Giotto's work apart from the work of other previous painters is the range of human emotions he showed both in faces and gestures. In the fresco, the Flight from Egypt, he shows Mary and Joseph, but he also shows people on the road gossiping as they pass.

THE MEDICI FAMILY

The powerful members of the Medici Family were influential in Florence beginning in the 1400s. They began as bankers and patrons of the arts. They had refined tastes and recognized the talent of the many great artists who were working in Florence at that time.

MEDICI FAMILY

Cosimo de' Medici

They used their personal prosperity to invest in artists and to further the cause of the humanist movement. In 1434, Cosimo de Medici gained the position of the head of Florence's city-state, so the Medici family continued to grow in their influence as rulers of Florence.

THE DOME OF THE FLORENCE CATHEDRAL

In 1418 AD, the rulers of Florence had a huge problem they had been ignoring for many years. They had a hole in the top of their cathedral because no one could figure out how to build a dome there.

Florence Cathedral

The dome would have to be 150 feet across and 180 feet above the ground. It was an enormous architectural and engineering challenge. They announced a contest with a prize of 200 gold coins in Florentine money called florins.

A hot-tempered man by the name of Filippo Brunelleschi who was a goldsmith by trade said he knew how to solve the problem by building two domes, one nested inside the other. He didn't want to give away too much about his idea because he was afraid it would be stolen.

In 1420, after much discussion, the rulers began to see that this strange man was a genius. They appointed him as the overseer of the project. There were many problems throughout the project, but when it was completed the dome was a masterpiece and it signaled the power and beauty that the Renaissance brought to the world for generations to come.

THE NEW IDEAS
BEGAN TO SPREAD

The new ideas of humanism and the styles of art this philosophy inspired quickly became known in the other prosperous city-states of Italy such as Rome as well as Milan and Venice. This early stage of the Renaissance is sometimes called the Italian Renaissance.

As the country of Italy became more prosperous, the people and culture were more progressive and their new way of life spread to the rest of the European countries. This time in history still inspires writers and artists today.

Italian Renaissance Art

Awesome! Now you know more about the beginning of the golden age of the Renaissance. You can find more Renaissance books from Baby Professor by searching the website of your favorite book retailer.

Visit
BABY PROFESSOR
EDUCATION KIDS
www.BabyProfessorBooks.com
to download Free Baby Professor eBooks
and view our catalog of new and exciting
Children's Books